"Dreaming, talking, and planning are important, but you only become better and realize life change, by taking action."

- Mike Rodriguez

NOW
IS THE BEST TIME

Stop Talking. Start Doing.

2019

Copyright © 2019
Tribute Publishing, LLC
Frisco, Texas

Tribute Publishing, LLC

Now is the Best Time
First Edition February 2019

All Worldwide Rights Reserved
ISBN: 978-0-9982860-0-6

All Rights Reserved. No part of this book may be reproduced, stored in a retrieval system, or transmitted, in any form, or by any means, electronic, mechanical, recorded, photocopied, or otherwise, without the prior written permission of the copyright owner or the Author, except by a reviewer who may quote brief passages in a review.

Printed in the United States of America.

In God We Trust.

"Let your actions overshadow your fears."
- Mike Rodriguez

CONTENTS

Introduction v

Chapter 1 – What's Important to You?........................ 1

Chapter 2 – What Are You Focused On? 15

Chapter 3 – What's Holding You Back?................... 31

Chapter 4 – Where Do You Start?.............................. 43

Chapter 5 – Why NOW Is the Best Time................ 61

Chapter 6 – Keep Remembering WHY Not WHAT
.... 79

Chapter 7 – I Challenge You.. 91

Conclusion 103

About the Author 107

Introduction

Most of us have a dream, a goal or something in our lives that we feel called to do. Are you feeling regret for not acting on something or giving up too soon? Are you going to miss out on a future opportunity if you fail to take action now? Or are you at the point where you are writing off what you need to do as not possible or not the right time?

If you answered yes to any of these, then you are not alone. But don't misunderstand me, I don't feel sorry for you. I'm not being mean; I'm being truthful. Having pity for you or you having pity on yourself won't help you to take action. My goal is for you to overcome your self-doubt and to recognize and own what you can do and why you need to do it, so you can avoid pity and regret. That's what this book is about.

I have concluded that there are several core reasons why people do not take the appropriate action to change or to pursue their big goals. Yes, you can make BIG changes in your life. But each time you pursue change or a dream, you might face doubt or fear that they won't be able to happen for you. As a result, they might not happen. It's not that they can't, but since you don't believe, you won't take the required action to make them real. I can tell you that change is indeed scary and uncomfortable, but you need to act. You must believe and stay the course, by remembering your purpose.

Some people act in spite of their life's issues, education or deficiencies, while others do not act in line with their created self-limiting beliefs.

You can start today by living your life with a philosophy of taking action **NOW** in all of the things that can impact your life. Over time, you can change your direction, make course corrections, and realize different outcomes. Your mind is what drives your actions, based on your beliefs, which ultimately leads you to your desired results.

In this book, I challenge you to evaluate yourself, to be honest about where you are going. The truth is that **you are indeed capable of becoming more, the profound question is: why aren't you? What is holding you back?** In almost every case, the answer is "YOU." You might not be in the best place right now in your career, health, relationships, marriage, friendships, finances, walk with God, or something else but you can improve your mindset and improve your situation.

You might be at a point where you need to change something in your life. You can eliminate a bad habit, or start accomplishing a big life goal, as long as you have faith, the right mindset, skillset, and take appropriate action. I promise you.

This book was written to allow you to evaluate your life and determine why you aren't going where you need to go. How much can you grow? Stop talking about it and start taking action NOW!

- **Mike Rodriguez**
  Author

"Each day you must do a little bit more,
and you will start to become
a little bit better."

- Mike Rodriguez

For Bonnie,
Thank you for being a never-ending support
and believing in me through all of my NOWS.

"When you figure out what's important in your life, you'll remove the things that aren't."

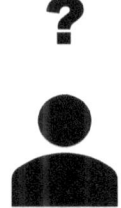

Chapter 1
What's Important to You?

Chapter 1 – What's Important to You?

Those who only dream are only dreamers, those who take action become.

I heard a story about a man in a small town who had been in love with a woman since he was a young boy. Now that he was a little older, his love had grown, and he knew that he wanted to marry her. There was only one problem, a big one; He was afraid to approach her. Because of his fear, he devised what he believed to be a strategic plan to win her love. Every day he would write a letter to her proclaiming his love. He would seal the letter and send it via certified mail to ensure that his written words would arrive directly in her hands. He was convinced that his loyalty, dedication, and heartfelt words would capture her heart. He knew that someday, eventually, he would win her over and marry her.

After a year of sending his love letters, he finally found the courage do what was ultimately necessary. He decided to go to the woman's house and ask her to marry him.

He was ready. He arrived at her home holding a beautiful bouquet of flowers. He took a deep breath, knocked on the door, and waited. Suddenly the door opened and standing in her doorway was the mailman. The man learned that after 12 months of personally delivering the letters to the woman, the mailman and the woman had fallen in love. They had gotten married.

This story covers the essential components which are needed for you to get the type of outcome required to succeed in your endeavors. It also highlights the problem areas that prevent success and led him to a less than desirable outcome:

Chapter 1 – What's Important to You?

1. The man was a dreamer, not a doer.
2. He was emotionally interested, but not fully committed.
3. He procrastinated due to fear and doubt.
4. He confused activity with productivity.
5. He focused on the wrong thing (writing).
6. He didn't know what was really important to him and finally,
7. He failed to take the right take action NOW.

Because of all of this, when he finally found the courage to act, it was too late. His delay had cost him. He didn't do want he needed to do, and someone else did. Some people act in spite of their fear, doubt, life's issues, education or deficiencies. Others will not act, keeping in line with their created self-limiting beliefs, and give in to fear and doubt. If you don't know what's important to you, I can assure you that you are probably focusing on the wrong things in your life as well. If you are focusing on the wrong things, you are getting the wrong results or maybe not the best results. Maybe you are losing out on your opportunity to someone else.

There is a critical risk that you must come to terms with and understand: **Something in your life is being neglected when you give attention to the wrong things.**

The question you must ask yourself is "Can I live with the consequences that I will be faced with by neglecting what is important to me?" The first thing for you to address is knowing and understanding what is important in your life.

Chapter 1 – What's Important to You?

You need to know what is truly important, what it will cost you to pursue it, and what it costs you to neglect it; Not just what you have and where you are, but what you need to do and where you need to go. This concept is what will lead you to take the appropriate action to start making progress and get your desired outcome.

There are many stories about people who took action, failed, kept going and finally realized their biggest dreams. There are also many stories of people who quit, got started again and went on to realize success. They did this after overcoming many obstacles that would frighten and paralyze most people. Unfortunately, the truth is that no one ever remembers those who just go through life, talking about what could have been; those who had the potential but didn't do anything with it.

Is that you?

Through your journey of a mindset of NOW, you can quickly learn that:

You must pursue what is important in your life. You must remove the things that aren't important in order to attain the things that are. You must focus on solutions, not excuses.

These concepts need to apply to you in a big way.

Chapter 1 – What's Important to You?

In your life you have been, are being, and will be faced with decisions that will impact your direction. Most people will not understand your dreams, actions, and decisions, and that is okay. But unlike me when I was younger, I encourage you to seek wise counsel, not misguided advice when faced with a difficult life-impacting decision. This means that you will need to talk with those who can help you on your journey. Don't seek out those who are only interested in approving what you want to do or telling you what you want to hear. Listen to experienced mentors so you can gain the wisdom that you will need on your journey. Learn from those who can help you to make the best decisions that will lead to the best possible outcomes.

What seems like a great idea today, may cost you in the future. Personal maturity will prompt you to seek sound advice and cause you to listen to what you **know** is best. Personal gain and selfish wants will prompt you to do what you **feel** is best. Reckless people seek advice only from those who will tell them what they want to hear, so they can justify their poor actions and decisions. Talking with friends about your career and life choices can be risky because most friends don't want to jeopardize your relationship. Most of them will encourage you regardless of the outcome. After all, it's not their life on the line. Their goal is usually about pushing you to 'pursue your happiness' or what 'makes you happy' to keep balance in the friendship. This wrong mindset will almost certainly lead to a poor quality of life, causing you to live well below your potential.

Chapter 1 – What's Important to You?

Know that happiness usually follows when you fulfill your calling, so **you should always run from someone who tells you to do what makes you happy.**

Your life goal should be to live a good quality of life, in line with your potential, with a track record of minimal regrets. Time and time again, history reveals that this is how you will have the greatest impact on other lives, and often, happiness and wealth follow this difficult path.

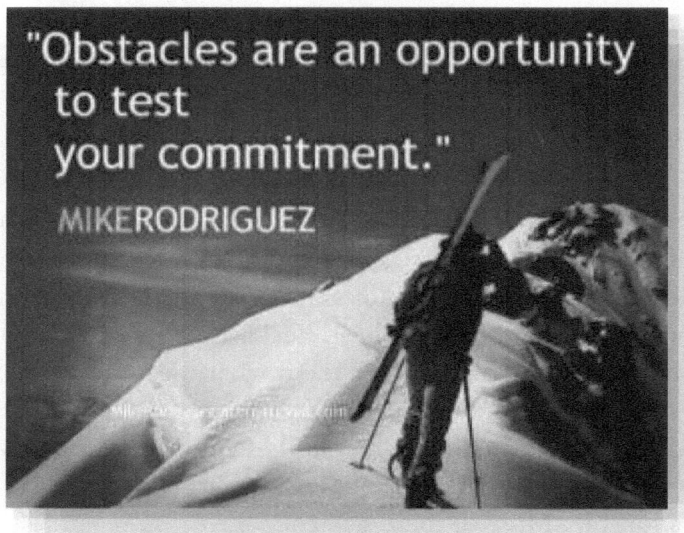

In order to become better in your life, you need to figure out what is important in your life, and that can be tricky. Excuses can get in the way and behaviors caused by years of routines can convince us that what used to be important is no longer important, or that what isn't

Chapter 1 – What's Important to You?

important, but enjoyable, IS important. In summary, most of us have a hard time separating what we 'want' to do from what we 'need' to do. This concept is the starting point for getting out of your own way.

Let's face it, we are selfish people by nature and when we 'want what we want,' we can fool ourselves into believing what we 'want' is what we 'NEED.' This is the deception that can keep you bound to mediocrity.

Opportunity Cost

Opportunity cost is the basic concept of what the important opportunity that you are pursuing will cost you. It is easily said but is difficult for most people to be honest about. Honesty with myself means that I should do what I NEED to do, which is usually the right and best thing, versus what I WANT to do, which is usually emotionally driven towards temporary gratification.

Every important opportunity that you pursue is going to cost you. This is why you need to know what is truly important to you. You are going to need to give up something, or I should say that you are already giving up something in order to get what you desire. The key point is that you must be clear in knowing what you are giving up and what it costs you. Sit down and evaluate where you are putting your time, energy and words. If you want to grow, it will cost you by giving up something that is holding you back. If you are not growing, it already costs you because you are neglecting what is important.

Chapter 1 – What's Important to You?

If something is truly important to you, you will get started now. If it isn't, you will probably never start, or you'll quit when things get too tough.

WANTS

Wants are very different than needs. You might want to be happy, loved, to be in a better relationship, to have more money, better career, to be famous or you might want something else. None of these things are bad to want unless it is for the wrong reasons, but the big question is, are you taking action to pursue those things and for the right reason? Are you making your 'wants' come true and if so, what is it costing you?

'Wants' are usually emotionally important to us, but we often find that for most 'wants' **we are usually more in love with the idea of the 'want' than we are with actually taking action to pursue the difficult challenge to make our 'want' a reality**.

Turning a want into a purpose is a big step that requires us to "become more." We must focus on how we can change ourselves to fit the outcome that we desire. For example, if you want a better job and you want more money, the first questions I would ask you are:

- What personal development are you taking NOW? and
- What actions are you taking NOW to prepare yourself for a better job?

Chapter 1 – What's Important to You?

The reason why I would ask these questions is because **if you aren't taking action to improve your skills now, then you aren't building value to yourself for your current employer or any other employer.**

If you aren't taking action to improve yourself now and you do get promoted, you probably won't appreciate where you are, or you won't perform well. If you aren't taking action now, you need to understand that you are only in love with the idea of being promoted, without taking on the responsibilities of improving yourself to actually get promoted. Your lack of action validates that it is not important to you. You would need to reconcile the truth that being promoted isn't important to you because as a matter of fact, you aren't doing anything to make yourself promotable. The reality is that you are only waiting for someone to promote you, and that is called being lazy. This complacent mindset will ultimately lead to lower results, create resentment and will cause you to develop a false perspective of being treated unfairly.

The second questions I would ask you are:
- **How do you currently view your money?**
- **How do you currently manage your money?**

If you 'want' money and view it as something to attain, you will never appreciate it, because **if you cannot effectively manage your level of income now, you will not manage it at a higher level.**

Chapter 1 – What's Important to You?

If you view money as an asset, as a product of your performance, and as a resource that is directly tied to your work results, work ethic, business value, and skill, then you will treat it responsibly when you earn more. **Money is a resource, and YOU define how you manage it. Money is never meant to define who you are.**

NEEDS

Needs are different than wants. Where wants are created from an emotionally charged desire, needs are typically birthed from either a pain of what is not happening in your life, a pain from what is happening that isn't indicative of your results, or a deeper calling inside of you that you know you must pursue for a bigger purpose. Needs will feel non-negotiable to you, but there is a catch: needs should propel you to take purposeful action.

(Be careful and do not take desperate action!)

You might want to have food to eat, want to be promoted, or you might want to go on a vacation, but when your healthy 'wants' turn to healthy 'needs,' they will fuel you to take purposeful action that aligns with the desired steps required to get the desired outcomes. Sometimes needs are so intense that when they are delayed or overlooked, the person will take the wrong action. This is unhealthy.

Chapter 1 – What's Important to You?

Early on in my life, I recognized that I needed to change my life in a big way. Previously I had 'wanted' change to happen, but it wasn't happening. I wasn't making it happen. But when I 'needed' to change, due to experiencing personal pain, I continued to take big action to change because it was now very important. I had purpose!

When I started my new course of change, I noticed that many people didn't understand and therefore, they questioned me or criticized me. **The reason they didn't understand why I was pursuing my dream, is because it wasn't their dream.** Of course, they wouldn't understand. Why would they?

The truth is that I am called to be my best and to do my best and so are you. Use your pain in a healthy way to push you to start, not to propel you away.

Even today, I still need to be productive and see that I am using and pursuing my full potential. I consider it to be a testament of my faith. I don't need to prove anything to anyone, but I know God is watching me and He is expecting me to follow the plans He has placed in my life. Christ is important to me, my wife and family are important to me, and my calling is important to me to inspire others and help them to succeed. Because I know this, I work to keep these things first and eliminate the things that aren't important. I know that I 'need' to live for these things, so I do.

What about you?

Chapter 1 – What's Important to You?

Challenge Questions:

What is important to you?
_____
_____
_____

What is important for you to give up?
(Stop doing)
_____
_____

What is important for you to pursue?
(Start doing)
_____
_____

What do you need to live for?
_____
_____

What is not important to you that you are allowing in your life?
_____
_____

Chapter 1 – What's Important to You?

What is it costing you not to pursue your dreams, calling, goals or purpose?

_____
_____

What will it cost you to take action to pursue them?

_____
_____

Notes:

_____
_____
_____
_____
_____
_____
_____

Chapter 2 – What Are You Focused On?

"What you focus on is what you will follow."

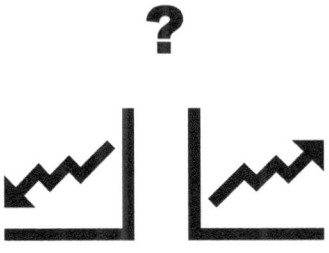

Chapter 2
What Are You Focused On?

Chapter 2 – What Are You Focused On?

Every day when you consider your available time, your value, and direction, you must understand that they all work together. They are influenced by your first interaction of the day which is with yourself. At the time your eyes open in the morning, you have started to establish your focus for the day. You have 24 hours to reinforce that focus, just like everyone else in the world, rich or poor, employed or unemployed, we all have 24 hours in a day. The next question then is, what are you focused on?

Some are focused on important things, and many are focused on many things, so it is true that some might have more tasks to focus on than others. That is a privilege that must be acknowledged. The unemployed person would love to be able to sit in traffic on his or her way to a job. The parent who has lost a child, would jump at the chance to chauffer the kids to school, pack lunches, and do laundry. It's all relative to how you choose to look at your life and your circumstances.

The point is, what you start focusing on affects how you view your life and how you live your days. Your viewpoint on your life drives the very first interactions with yourself every morning. These things will heavily influence how you see your day, why you do what you do, and what you are going to do to become better.

For many of us, our problems are a direct result of what we chose to do or not do and how we choose to do them. This has an impact on how we wake up in the morning and can create a domino effect of chaos if we aren't focused on productivity. Then, as we start to go through our daily routines, things probably won't

Chapter 2 – What Are You Focused On?

work out like we want, creating a vicious circle. Your routines can be very dangerous if they are taking you in the wrong direction!

You can become falsely conditioned to believe that in your life you are a just along for the ride or you might believe you are a victim of circumstances. You might accept that you are just a player in the game and that you are destined to repeat the same behaviors or even bad behaviors that have been part of your life. Take ownership and take action!

When you wake up in the morning, the first thing you should do when you interact with yourself is to avoid the temptation to think or say anything negative. Focus on the positives and create a new direction. Think about or say something positive! Are you alive? That is awesome! Are you employable? Perfect! Start with being thankful for what you already DO HAVE that you might be overlooking or taking for granted instead of focusing on what you DON'T have or want. **You must appreciate where you are and what you have before you can go where you need to go and have more.**

If you usually say, "Here we go again," which is negative, this will cause your mind to start focusing on a standard "negative" outcome. This is an unhealthy driver for the rest of your day. Instead, program yourself to say **"Good morning! I am alive, and I'm thankful for what I have. Opportunity awaits me, and it is up to me!"** Initially, this may seem silly to you, but think of it this way: If you aren't saying

Chapter 2 – What Are You Focused On?

something positive then you are in fact saying something negative, and how silly is that? Especially when you consider that YOU are the one impacting your day and your own life negatively.

Another way we lose focus is by looking at what others have. Sometimes we desire the lives or possessions of others, or we might live to become like or outperform someone else.

In the 2016 Olympics, Chad Le Clos was faced with the reality that he would face his rival Michael Phelps to a rematch in the 200m butterfly event. Previously in 2012, Le Clos had beat Phelps and won the gold. Shortly after that event, Phelps announced that he was retiring. Only a short period later, Phelps would announce to the world that he would be entering the 2016 Olympics because he concluded that the swimmers had gotten slow. Le Clos was offended by the remark, but Phelps was driven because he meant what he said. Up to and during the event, Le Clos trash talked Phelps. It was apparent that Le Clos was bothered by his rival and his feelings were getting the best of him.

The day of the event was intense. The two swimmers squared off and prepared to start the race. At the signal to start, the race commenced, and both swimmers took to the water. During the race, an amazing thing happened that few would notice. It was only after photographs surfaced afterward revealing the truth behind the 'visions' that were driving each swimmer. It was very clear in the image that blatantly showed everyone that:
- Michael Phelps was swimming purposefully, with his head directly facing forward and his eyes rigidly set on his goal.

Chapter 2 – What Are You Focused On?

- Chad Le Clos was also swimming, but his head was turned towards Michael Phelps. His eyes purposefully set on his opponent.

The end result?
Phelps won. Le Clos lost.

Why did Le Clos lose? Clearly, Michael Phelps was focused on himself, getting to the finish line fast, and winning the Gold. He was committed to winning the race and went in with that mindset.

Le Clos, on the other hand, was focused on beating Michael Phelps, which is a negative driver. **Phelps was focused on his goal**, a positive driver. Phelps was in control of pursuing it, and he attained it. Le Close was focused on the wrong thing, Phelps, and it cost him.

Chapter 2 – What Are You Focused On?

What your mind focuses on, your eyes will follow and what your eyes follow your mind will focus on.

You might not be an Olympic swimmer, but you are in the race of life, with an expectation to win the prize at the end. What is the prize you might ask? Well, you need to figure that out for yourself and quickly. Are you focused on the prize at the end, or are you distracted by other things that are temporarily interesting, maybe satisfying to you at the moment? Are you living your life to compete with someone else? Are you living your life in envy of what others are doing? Or are you living to become the best YOU?

I have found that when my mind wanders, and I focus on others, my eyes lose focus and my mind and body disengage on my life. It is probably the same for you. When this happens, you obviously cannot perform at your best, but you also must consider and understand the consequences. When we focus short term, we usually get short term results that might not help us to get to our established long-term goals. The key here is to be able to understand 'Why' you are doing what you are doing and 'What' the benefits are for you, and others. What are the benefits if you continue to pursue and attain the end goal that is important to you? The reason this is critical is because if you are pursuing a goal that is not that important to you or isn't really your goal, you face three major risks:

1. You might not ever get started
2. You won't give the full effort that is required
3. You will probably quit when things get too tough

Chapter 2 – What Are You Focused On?

The ultimate deception with all three of these risks is that when you face failure, you will falsely believe that there is something wrong with you or your abilities, which might cause you to start blaming or making excuses. The truth is that when you are focused on the wrong things, you simply have the wrong mindset, so you deliver a very different result. This result is usually in line with your distracted focus and not in-line with your true goal or your true potential.

What about you?
- Do you know what you are focused on in your life?
- Can you say with complete honesty that you are focused on things that generate the best outcomes for you and your life?
- Would people close to you agree with you?
- Are you experiencing the outcomes you desire and are fully capable of attaining?
- Are you proud to announce that you are using your full potential by the way you are living your life?
- Are you living your life to become the best YOU based on your abilities and purpose, or
- Are you living to impress and compete with others?

Everyone should be able to evaluate these questions honestly, but there are only a few who can truthfully answer yes! Most who can are top performers in their lives, families, and careers. They aren't perfect, just focused.

I know some people who are embarrassed to say what they are focused on, and unfortunately, that is exactly why they do not change, and why they cannot succeed in their important endeavors. They are mentally bound to

Chapter 2 – What Are You Focused On?

mediocrity, deception and sometimes life-long failure. They are not committed to focusing on realizing their important goals because they see them as difficult or impossible. Sometimes it is not important to them, and other times it is because they just don't believe they can reach them. The truth is that **you simply cannot commit to something that you do not believe in.**

There are others who are indifferent about what they are focused on. They incorrectly view their life as just another day, living the same routines each day just to get through. They live under the deception that since all is okay, that they don't need to do anymore. Performance in life is very difficult for most people. When you factor in that the key components to a better quality of life are directly attributed to faith, purpose, skill level and the desire to work and take action, you need to realize that you better have razor sharp purpose and focus. The benefit to you here is that the more you focus, the more you engage. **Focusing can generate the most robust life for disciplined people, or it can create difficulties for those who don't understand.**

Some despise or maybe event hate change, even when they continue to do the same things, getting the same results, sometimes ruining their lives. There are others that want to excel in life, but they simply aren't willing to take the appropriate action to do what is required. They believe change to be silly or that a new life isn't meant for them. This is how I used to think.

It was only when I started to realize that my lack of progress in life was due to my lack of belief, leading to a lack

Chapter 2 – What Are You Focused On?

of focus. It was because I couldn't see myself as the man I needed to be and, I couldn't believe or accept that I could become more. I wasn't performing in life; therefore I wasn't getting positive results. Maybe I should say I was getting the wrong results. Fortunately, all of that was about to change, because my focus was about to change.

When I looked back on my life, I started to see that from the time I was in middle school until the adult years of my life, I had an uncanny ability to recognize a certain deficiency in myself and others. I realized that people, including myself, weren't accomplishing goals or getting things done simply because they weren't taking the appropriate action. The compelling question to me was always, why? The answer was clear; some were afraid while others didn't believe that the outcomes could happen for them. Others were focused on pursuing what they thought was best for them, or what others wanted them to do. They were settling in their lives and conditioning themselves to believe it was okay.

In my final year of high school and throughout my first years of college, I was starting to experience certain failures. I can say with complete honesty that it was very disappointing. Not because I couldn't accomplish the tasks that were being presented, but because I wasn't acting on the tasks with the level of effort required. I wasn't working within the time frame required so I could get a different and possibly better result. I was a victim of my own circumstances. For me, **I didn't want to be a part of the herd. I didn't think I was better than anyone else, but I knew that I was better than the results I was getting.**

Chapter 2 – What Are You Focused On?

I watched curiously and fearfully as people prepared themselves for their life's journey, not knowing where they were going and sometimes, going somewhere that they didn't really want to go. I didn't want to be like that. I also knew that as a young man, I was building my tempo for the rest of my life.

When I was a few years older and married my wife, I started to see the same, less than desirable outcomes. Not because I wasn't capable of changing the outcomes, but again because I wasn't taking the appropriate action. I wasn't learning from and acting on changing the outcomes. My marriage was important to me, and I was committed for the long haul, but I was focused on the short term. Many times, as my mind was looking at 'what' I wanted to do, my soul was pushing me to remember WHY I was married and focus on respect, collaboration, and commitment.

Your marriage or your relationship is also about commitment, respect, and unselfishness. However, if you are always focusing on your wants and not the needs of the marriage, you will follow the wrong path and get the results you are pursuing.

These same issues were also taking hold of my spiritual life. I wanted to be a better Christian, but I was focused on doing other things that were self-serving and required less discipline. These things weren't getting me anywhere, but they were taking me farther from being a better me and farther from my relationship with God. It was easy to say that I was a Christian, but without focusing on WHY I was a Christian and what that meant, I was lost and misdirected.

Chapter 2 – What Are You Focused On?

When I started working in the business world, I was fortunate to be hired by an organization that had established a healthy culture of performance. Yes, the company had employed imperfect people who faced challenges each day, but the main thing that stood out to me were the positive attitudes and performance-based focus of the team, in spite of the challenges they faced. Although most people around me were performing, I wasn't, and I could feel that I was dragging down myself and the team. My poor performance created a snowball effect. It had rolled into my business life from my personal life and was now rolling back into my personal life, causing problems for me in all facets of my world.

I felt terrible knowing that I wasn't a positive contributor and that I was fully capable of becoming one. I quickly realized that **if I wanted my results to change, then I needed to change.** The problem was that I just did not know where, how or when to start, and I kept coming up with what I thought were valid excuses not to start, so I just wasn't starting. I considered myself capable and smart; I just wasn't working with or towards my true potential. I had developed a bad habit of hanging around with a few individuals who also weren't performing in life or business, and I noticed that they complained quite a bit as well. They had an excuse for everything. They lived by excuses and a mindset of what they wanted to do, not what they needed to do, and I was following them. You could say that their blame, poor attitudes, and belief systems were out of control. Even though they were nice people, I no longer wanted to be part of their group or direction, so I took action to break away. I was decisive, and I made it happen.

At the time it was sad to lose friends and old routines, but the positive change was very liberating. I had decided to change what I was focusing on and as a result, my mind

Chapter 2 – What Are You Focused On?

followed. It caused me to take decisive actions that would start me on the path towards a better life. I'm not telling you to get rid of your friends, but if you have someone in your life that you care about, help them up, but don't let them drag you down. If you can't do this, because they don't want to, it might be time to move on and love them from a distance. **Your life is too important to compromise.**

Opportunities vs. Distractions

Through the process of changing your focus, you need to be able to differentiate between opportunities and distractions. Many people will want to help you, and you will want to pursue paths that might not get you to your destination. You will be presented with options in life that look very appealing, but that might not help you get to your final destination.

When you focus on a positive end result, you need to understand WHY you are doing what you are doing. If you don't have a great reason why, that is responsible, morally correct and beneficial, then you are probably facing a distraction, not an opportunity.

Opportunities are options that will challenge you and will ultimately help you to get you closer to your goals. Opportunities have risks, but they lead to reward.

Distractions on the other hand, usually don't challenge you, but they are usually emotionally driven, and this is what confuses some people. They also have risks, but the risks are usually detrimental. Engaging in distractions can

Chapter 2 – What Are You Focused On?

and will create delays. Sometimes temporarily and sometimes long term. The time and attention you give to the distraction will inevitably lead to negative consequences, impacting your long-term goals and possibly your direction. Unlike distractions which take from us and prevent us from growing, opportunities benefit us and help us to grow.

Opportunities are challenging and require you to challenge yourself.

Distractions might require effort, but they are usually counterproductive when all is said and done.

When you are presented with a new situation, take time to evaluate it and decide if it is an opportunity or a distraction. If you are being rushed to enter into a situation, you might ask yourself why you are being rushed. Seek to understand who is benefiting and what the consequences and benefits are of making your decision.

Opportunities will be presented as challenges that require effort and demand that you grow to meet them. Make sure that you know what you are focused on and that you know and understand the benefits and risks.

If something looks too good to be true and isn't aligned with your best interests, then it is probably a distraction.

Chapter 2 – What Are You Focused On?

What about you?

- Are you focused on what you aren't able to do or will you focus on how to find a way?
- Do you focus on the reasons why you can't, or will you focus on why you can and should take action?
- Do you focus on the negatives or do you seek to find the positives?
- Do you focus on what the outcomes can be in your life or do you focus what you think they will be?

Challenge Questions:

What are you focused on?

_____
_____
_____

Where will that focus get you?

_____
_____

What do you need to start focusing on?

_____
_____

Chapter 2 – What Are You Focused On?

Where can that focus take you?

_____
_____

What things distract you from focusing on what's important to you?

_____
_____

What will it cost you to follow a distraction?

_____
_____

Why?

_____
_____

Notes:

_____
_____
_____
_____
_____
_____
_____

Chapter 2 – What Are You Focused On?

Chapter 3 – What's Holding You Back?

"There are many things in life
that will hold you back. You believing them
will be the biggest one."

Chapter 3
What's Holding You Back?

Chapter 3 – What's Holding You Back?

You should never say "I can't." These words are defeating and self-limiting at the least, and self-destructive at the most. The issue with saying negative or self-limiting words is not actually the words. The issue is that when you say these words, your mouth is actually expressing what your own mind already believes. That should frighten you.

As we continually confess the phrase "I can't!" we are in effect reinforcing a negative belief which in turn becomes our own reality. It is cyclical.

In summary, we believe what we keep telling ourselves, then we live our own limitations, and it's never okay to be okay with that. **Put good stuff into your head.**

In my live seminars, I usually share a story about a little boy who gets to see an elephant at the circus for the first time. As the story goes, the little boy diligently watches the elephant all day as the elephant lifts thousands of pounds of material to build the circus tent. The elephant is extremely strong, and the little boy is certainly impressed by the elephant's strength. At the end of the day, the trainer leads the elephant back to his pen and then proceeds to tie a small rope around the elephant's leg. With the other end of the rope, the trainer ties it to a small wooden stake and pushes the peg into the ground. When the little boy sees the large and powerful elephant tied to the small rope and the fragile wooden stake, he confronts the trainer. The boy tells the trainer that the elephant is super strong and can easily break free from the small rope and peg restraining him.

The trainer then talks to the boy and lets him know that indeed the elephant is very strong and yes, the elephant

Chapter 3 – What's Holding You Back?

could break free from the rope if he believed he could. The trainer then shares with the boy that the elephant does not believe that he can break free. When the boy asks the trainer why, the trainer reveals his answer.

The trainer tells that boy that since the elephant was a baby, not much bigger than the little boy, he had restrained the elephant with the very small rope. Through many years of attempting to break free without success, the elephant had grown up believing that he could not break free; therefore he stopped attempting to break free.

Although you are not an elephant, the same limiting concept applies to you, if you accept limitations. What you believe is what you will follow. If you have grown up believing you cannot do something because you were told that you cannot, then that is your rope. If you failed at something once and then accepted that outcome as permanent, then that is your rope.

Chapter 3 – What's Holding You Back?

The key here is that you must understand that the rope is not created during the failure to get your desired outcome, the rope is created when we believe that the desired outcome is permanent for us.

Once the rope is set, the mind is convinced and will establish that belief as a new standard. The mouth then conveys what the mind has decided to believe, usually announcing the limitation as

"I can't" or "it's not possible."

The deception here is that not only are these statements false, but the mind must continually believe them in order to justify the lack of action. The mouth must state and claim the limitation as 'impossible,' so that others will not attempt what we say is impossible. This allows us to justify our inability to act on what we say is impossible. It is important to understand this concept for a few reasons:

1. When you say "I can't" you are reinforcing a negative belief that you have created.
2. When others say "It's impossible," that's simply what THEY believe. That doesn't mean it's true for you.

The strategy here is to change your limiting beliefs and look beyond what you see. Ask yourself:

- Why do I believe I can't?
- Is there another way?
- Have I grown to be able to work through my challenge now?
- Has my skillset changed or does it need to change for me to be able to get a new result?

Chapter 3 – What's Holding You Back?

Just because something didn't work for you initially, doesn't mean that it won't work for you permanently.

Whether you are applying for college, a job, taking medicine for a sickness, or asking someone out on a date, you stand a chance of facing rejection. When you take action to do something and encounter failure, or when the answer is no, you must understand that the answer NO does not mean that the long-term solution is no for you. 'No,' in these instances simply means you cannot proceed down that particular path. You can still keep moving; you just need to find another way.

If you apply for a job and they say no, it doesn't mean you can't get a job, you can still apply for other jobs; you just cannot work there. If you take meds and don't get well, it doesn't mean you can't get well. Those meds aren't for you, but you can still seek other ways to pursue getting well. If you apply for college or ask someone out and they say no, it doesn't mean that you cannot go to college or date. Again, you simply cannot go to THAT college or date THAT person. Do you get the concept?

Likewise, when you start towards a new goal or a new opportunity in life and encounter failure, you must keep going and find another way.

Don't give up on your goal, find a new way to get to it.

Chapter 3 – What's Holding You Back?

COMMITMENT vs. INTEREST

Most people encounter failure because they never give the efforts necessary to get the best results. They usually give the efforts they want to give based on their level of commitment (which is usually not that high), and then complain deflecting the blame to others.

If you have an interest in something, that means it is on your radar, but you haven't decided to give what is necessary for the best outcome. If you are only interested in something, you are in the EXPLORATORY stage. This is very different than being committed which means you are in the ACTION stage. You should have an interest in something prior to being committed, but you need to make sure you are fully committed when you take action. Most people who only show interest in something will not fully follow through with what is required to succeed, due to some of the concepts we have already talked about. A task or goal might not be that important to you, or you might not be focused on the potential benefits that are being presented to you.

When you decide that the task is important to you, your interest moves to involvement based on your level of commitment.

Your level of success will then be determined by these items working together:

- **Your level of interest**
- **Your level of commitment**
- **Your level of involvement**
- **The actions you choose to take to sustain long-term success.**

Chapter 3 – What's Holding You Back?

These concepts are meant to help you determine what is important to you, and to help you to understand:

- **WHY you are interested**
- **WHAT level of involvement you will take**
- **WHEN you are going to take action**
- **HOW you will accomplish the task at hand**

You Aren't Your Deficiency

A few years back I was talking with a friend who wanted to publish a story. He said that the topic of the story was going to be about his codependency and the struggles that he was facing. Towards the end of the conversation, I curiously asked him if he had considered a name for the book. "Yes," he said, "I would like to call it Larry's Co-Dependency." I immediately responded. "Larry, I cannot let you call your book Larry's Codependency." He curiously replied, "Why?"

I said, "Because, codependency is not WHO you ARE, it has been WHAT you have been DOING." He quickly asked me to elaborate.

I asked him about the day he was born, and I had him inventory who was with him. "My mom," he said. "No, I responded, "Your mom delivered you. She was as a vessel for you to come into the world, but she was not with you. The proof is that they had to carry you to her arms physically. You were born as one, and only God was with you." I then asked him to give me an inventory of what he was born with when he came into this world.

Chapter 3 – What's Holding You Back?

This is the list that we agreed on that he possessed the day of his birth:
- A brain for thinking, and function
- Two eyes to see
- Two ears to listen
- A nose to smell and breath
- A mouth to eat, talk and breath
- 2 Arms and 2 hands to lift and grasp
- 2 legs and two feet to walk, run and stand
- A digestive system
- A waste disposal system
- A respiratory system
- A reproductive system, and
- A heart.

We also agreed that if a person was born without these things, then that is the way God needed them to be for their journey.

After we accepted that God had made him and equipped him to be fully prepared to succeed in this world, I asked him about his flesh tag. "Flesh tag" he inquired? "Yes," I said, you know the one that God gave you that said "Codependent" on it?

"Mike, I have all of the things we talked about, but I don't have a flesh tag of codependency."

"You are right Larry, you don't," I said. "God gave you everything you need to succeed in this world, except for that. YOU added that. With this truth, you can know with clear certainty that codependency is not WHO you ARE, but only WHAT you have been doing. So, now you can stop claiming it as yours."

Chapter 3 – What's Holding You Back?

This is a true conversation that was life-changing for this man, and this truth can be life changing for you too. If you have an addiction, a bad habit, an unhealthy routine, a personality trait, a person, or an issue that you brought into your life, the issue isn't yours to claim; the issue is yours to manage through and let go. I'm not saying that you should shirk responsibilities for what you do because you shouldn't. What I am saying is that what is not on the previous list isn't supposed to be in your life. It was picked up by you and added to your life somewhere along your journey. Now you need to take action to start getting rid of it and let it go.

For me, I personally started a bad habit of drinking too much alcohol when I was in Corporate America. Eventually, the routine of drinking turned into a solid problem that I needed to address. I quickly had to come to terms with the fact that the way I was drinking was completely holding me back in my life. It was preventing me from becoming the husband, father, friend, person, and follower of Christ that I needed to be. I was starting to feel the pain, and so I concluded that I was the one who brought drinking into my life, so I was the one who needed to take action to remove it. In my situation, I turned it over to God, and He took it away.

Through the years I have had this discussion with many people, and some say "Oh, Mike you are an alcoholic." "No," I calmly and confidently proclaim. The truth that I live and accept is that I am not an alcoholic. I don't claim that tag, and no, I am not in denial. I understand that I don't do well with alcohol, but I also don't do well with chocolate almond ice cream. Abusing alcohol is something that **I used to do, and I no longer DO that**. It was never who I am and

Chapter 3 – What's Holding You Back?

will never be how I identify myself. I am not that title, and I wasn't born with that. It simply isn't mine. I picked it up, and I gave it to God and let it go. He doesn't call me by that descriptor, he calls me by my name.

Some have said that I am in denial. They are wrong. That is what they want to believe and what they want me to be, but the proof is in the results: Through the grace of God, I have been sober now for many years. I have no interest in adding alcohol back into my life, nor will I ever. I can say that with full and complete commitment because I know who I am.

Who are you?

What do you claim?

When you claim something to be yours that isn't part of you; the risk is that you then falsely let it become yours, and you let it become a part of you. You might have a disease that has suddenly shown up inside of your body. Don't claim it. Fight it and give it to God. It might win the battle, and it might not. The outcome is not up to you to know, but it is up to you to stand up and fight for your life.

Remember YOUR points to proclaim:
- What I DO isn't WHO I am.
- I will Stop DOING the wrong things
- I will Stop claiming deficiencies as 'WHO I am'
- I will start removing unhealthy things from my life that I DO
- I will start replacing them with GOOD things
- I will not let negative TAGS hold me back.

Chapter 3 – What's Holding You Back?

Challenge Questions:

What is holding you back?

_____
_____
_____

Why?

_____
_____

What do you need to start doing to break free?

_____
_____

How will you remove your limitations?

_____
_____

What things cause you to say I CANT?

_____
_____

What have you been falsely saying you are?

_____
_____

Chapter 3 – What's Holding You Back?

Why?

_____
_____

Notes:

_____
_____
_____
_____
_____
_____

> "When you fail to take action,
> you are destined to fail."

Chapter 4
Where Do You Start?

Chapter 4 – Where Do You Start?

I was having a conversation with a friend about one of his team members that wasn't using his full potential. He informed me that this person was always doing things that were counter-productive. They were consistently giving excuses about why they weren't accomplishing the things that needed to be completed. "Mike," he said, "this person has their priorities out of order. I laughed and responded, "No, you are incorrect. They have their priorities in order; they simply have them prioritized in an order important to them. You just don't like the order." (He didn't like my answer either)

This is also a complex subject that partners with 'wants and needs.' When it comes to us as people, you must understand that most of us don't want to change and we won't, unless we experience some kind of pain. However, we can change when understanding the potential risks of our actions and the possible benefits of prioritizing. The ultimate goal for you is to figure out your ultimate goal or goals. The thing or things that contribute to your ultimate quality of life.

What is it that you:

1. Need to do NOW that is life or business impacting?
2. Need to get done, but maybe not today
3. Want to do, but might keep you from being productive?

Go for it.
Don't be afraid of making the wrong decision, be more afraid of making no decision.

Chapter 4 – Where Do You Start?

Early in my career, I was in sales in Dallas in the telecom industry. I viewed my job as just a way to make ends meet, so I drove to work each day, did what I thought I was supposed to do, and then I would drive home at night and do family related or friend-related activities. My life was complacent and very unproductive; however, I would have never acknowledged that back then. The reality is, I was never starting because I didn't know where to start.

One Monday, it was another hot and dry day in Dallas, and I was behind on my quota again. I was out working hard, or so I thought. I was scouting my territory for what I believed to be the best area for gaining new prospects. That week I had enough of being on the phone making calls. My colleagues and I (also underperformers), had decided that phone prospecting just didn't work anymore, that it was outdated. I had also come to the solid conclusion that prospective clients just weren't engaged this week. Because of my conclusions, I had jumped in my car and was out in Dallas working 'hard.' In all honesty, I wasn't doing anything work-related at all. I was merely just driving around losing money by burning gas (and my motivation) while deceiving myself that I was working. Realistically, I had to get out of the office because it exposed the fact that I didn't have any new meetings to attend, and I needed to hide that ugly truth.

As I drove around, I came to terms with the fact that I had to do something, but I just couldn't get myself to get started. Every time I decided to make a follow-up call or to drop in on a prospect, I would convince myself that it just wasn't the right time. I would tell myself that they wouldn't be in or that they wouldn't be interested in talking with me.

Chapter 4 – Where Do You Start?

I had become very good at fooling everyone: my boss, my team and myself (or so I thought). I had many excuses; I believed them and could share them passionately! I knew I needed a job, but my work wasn't important to me. I had not yet realized that **I wasn't hired to do a job, but rather to deliver results. This required me to grow,** but in order to do this, I knew I had to get started. But where?

Inevitably, that day, like many others, resulted in me making the one decision I always made. The decision to not start, again. I would usually just drive home and 'work from home,' but this day, on the way home, something happened that transformed my view of my job and my life. I stopped, pulled over and sighed. I genuinely asked myself:
- *Mike, why are you going home?*
- *What's going happen when you get there?*
- *Are you able to live with the results and consequences of your actions?*
- *Why aren't you getting started?*

I decided that I would be brutally honest with myself. So being brutally honest with myself, I declared that I was going home because:
- I feared the negativity and rejection of my job
- I lacked confidence
- I had created complacent routines
- I had succumbed to chronic procrastination
- I didn't know where to start

I also realized that when I got home, nothing work-related would happen at all, thus starting the cycle of no productivity all over again. I was coming to terms with the fact that up to

Chapter 4 – Where Do You Start?

this point in my career, I had created a great habit of working at 'not being productive,' and I was succeeding, by always believing and living out that 'Now, was just not the right time.' The problem that had developed was my flawed concept had created a habit of perpetually not starting. I was forced to come to terms with these facts:

1. I didn't like my horrible job results.
2. I had a wife and new baby that were relying on me.
3. I wasn't fooling myself anymore; I was 'on' to me.
4. I had created a mindset of avoiding becoming more.
5. I needed to start somewhere.

The truth is that **the pain of the consequences of my poor job performance had become important to me.**

I arrived at the deep realization that I had to put an end to this deceptive mindset madness of 'procrastination,' by simply taking a small step to 'start working.' I decided to start that day with an act that would break my routine.

I immediately pulled over to a small office building, went inside and I decided that I would make 5 cold calls. I knew 5 wasn't a big number, but it was bigger than the zero calls I was making. I found that it was a tough mental decision to follow through making the calls and those 5 were all that I could bear, but I did them, and it felt good. No sales results came out the calls, but a confidence boost was born. Those calls were tough to make, so I got back in my car and continued heading home. On the way, my desire called out to me again. "Keep starting!" So I took the next exit, stopped again and made 5 more calls in the next building. Nothing again, so back in the car, "Keep starting," then on to the next exit, into the next building, and 5 more calls.

I kept starting over and over, and finally, I set a new meeting. It was awesome! Getting started paid off. Throughout the entire struggle, I kept wanting to come up with excuses like
"I need more time to prepare,"
"Maybe now isn't the best time or place,"
"Maybe I should wait until I do more research,"
and other similar nonsense. The truth was that **the realization of the benefits of positive job performance had become apparent and had become important to me.**

    I evaluated the productivity of my taking action, and I was ecstatic. I also felt really stupid at the same time. It wasn't hard work, but I had let 'not knowing where to start' become hard work. I had been giving in to focusing on the wrong things and listening to the wrong people. I had been focused on the negativity of the activities and not the outcome of my productivity! I had been thinking like a poor performer, so I had become a poor performer, but not anymore.

    I made a decision that I would use this same technique the next day, and every day until I reached my desired goals. I knew that if I could change my mind and get started on the hardest thing, I could **focus on results, instead of activity, that would eventually get me better results.**

Chapter 4 – Where Do You Start?

I was right, my plan worked, and I started to succeed. However, through this process, I learned much about myself and about business and life in general.

I learned **10 rules required to succeed in life and business:**

1. What you believe is what you will follow. What do you believe? Why?
2. There is a difference between quitting and failing (I was quitting because I had never committed).
3. Failing helps me to learn how to succeed, as obstacles are an opportunity to test my commitment.
4. Long term success requires focusing on short term action and short-term results.
5. You must identify what is keeping you from starting.
6. Set and know your goals or you won't know where to go.
7. Persistent and consistent action leads to productive results.
8. Starting anywhere is better than not starting. You can always learn and adjust.
9. You must figure out what is important to you:
    a. What consequences you DON'T want to happen, and
    b. What benefits you DO want to gain.
10. You must take action NOW in order to succeed.

I learned to apply these rules to my life and to make my profession an art. Too serious or silly you might say? I would tell you that your life direction is serious business.

Chapter 4 – Where Do You Start?

It is sillier (and sadder) to live below your potential. I would also respond by saying that serious life results can only come from a committed person. Committed people know that their mindset drives their actions. These actions generate results and produce income, which ultimately finances your lifestyle and quality of life. Money isn't the greatest result, but it is an indicator of your mindset and career health.

Simply stated, **if you want better results, YOU need to become better.** The best time to start is now, the best place to start is with your 3 main categories: Your NEED to Do NOWs, Your Standards, and Your Wants.

NEED to Do NOW:

These are your Life Impacting tasks that will impact your life positively if acted on and negatively if neglected. These are your #1 items on your to-do list.

What is it that you NEED to do 'today' that can improve your quality of life, get you working towards your goals immediately and minimize your stress?

What have you been neglecting or what is required for you to act on today?

If you came home and found a certified letter from the IRS requiring you to call them, when would you call? If you received a call from your doctor asking you to come in quickly, when would you go? If your boss tells you they need to talk with you, when would you make it happen?
If you said NOW or ASAP, then you are correct. These items are what I call "life impacting" items and they require a sense of urgency to resolve NOW. They are as important as your big goals and dreams and should be treated with the same respect, attention, and sense of urgency.

Chapter 4 – Where Do You Start?

When we neglect these items, there are usually consequences to face that we usually cannot or are not able to live with. Needs are often neglected because they are difficult to start doing. They usually require effort, discipline, and mental effort or physical action. The goal that's calling out to you should be laced into this category.

The key to your Life Impacting NEEDS is that when you start on them, you will eventually feel better emotionally because you are being responsible. They require mental and physical involvement, and that is why we procrastinate with our critical needs. They have the greatest long-term payoff because of the hard work required to tackle them. We receive gratification by completing them and receiving the benefits of our work.

They also usually have the greatest consequences if neglected too long. Starting today, your big goals and dreams should be moved up in your life and categorized to "Life Impacting Needs," from being emotional "WANTs" For business and life-impacting matters, you can ask yourself:

- **If I choose not to act on this today, what are the consequences that I will face?**
- **Am I prepared to live with those consequences?**
- **If I choose to act today, what are the potential benefits I will gain?**
- **How can this help me in my life?**

You need to decide what it is that has been calling out to you to pursue. You know what it is, but you might be suppressing it to prevent yourself from taking action.

Chapter 4 – Where Do You Start?

Always start off your day doing your NEEDS first, so you can properly engage your mind.

Standards:
The important things that you have do every day, but can be pushed off tomorrow if necessary, are called Standards.

Standards are the second priorities of your day, and you should only start acting on them after you have completed or started on your NEEDS. Standards will vary from person to person but should be prioritized according to the level of:
1. Impact on your life (goal progress)
2. Importance to your life (less stress)
3. Ability to delay if necessary (won't create a negative consequence)

Wants:
The opposite of NEEDS, wants are not that important and will not impact our lives if we do not do them today. However, WANTS are the emotionally driven items that are fun, so they are mentally appealing to us.

Your 'Wants' are creating problems in your life today.
Here is why:
Instead of starting with NEEDS every day, most people do what they 'want' to do, because it is emotionally appealing and doesn't look like work.

The risk is that when you do what you 'want' to do, you are neglecting what you NEED to do. You are creating

Chapter 4 – Where Do You Start?

your own worry and stress. Before you engage in your daily activities, remember your big goals and evaluate your priorities. Ask yourself **Is what I'm about to do, going to taking me closer to my Big goals or will it take me further from them?** Then, be honest with yourself, and make a list that looks like this:

NEEDS	*STANDARDS*	*WANTS*
Pay that bill	Lunch with Mike	Facebook
Work out	Laundry	TV
Make that call	Time with kids	Nap
Exercise	Grocery store	Coffee w Sue

Remember, your list can and will change each day. What is life impacting today, might become a standard tomorrow and what is a 'want' today, might become life impacting in a few days. However, your big goals should always remain on your list, at the top. You need to see them so that you can act on them NOW!

Discipline Is the Key to NOW

Discipline is the art of taking action to do what is important instead of doing what isn't.

When you create a mindset of now, you are constantly reminding yourself WHY you are doing what you are doing, WHAT you will avoid by taking action and what the benefits will be to you and others close to you. Anything worthwhile in life is difficult to start, and discipline is the key to start the engine! Discipline is an easy mental concept with a complex component – action NOW.

Chapter 4 – Where Do You Start?

When you can start acting now, you start developing your discipline. Discipline also helps when you encounter this next obstacle.

FEAR

One of the most profound excuses that most of us have for not getting started is fear. When I ask people to describe fear for me, they can't. They usually describe a scary situation, but that isn't fear; it's a scary situation.

Can YOU describe fear?
What does it look like, smell like or sound like?

The truth is that fear doesn't possess any of those characteristics. No one, including you, has ever seen fear. You might have felt fearful, but it was probably in response to something you experienced that was frightening. **Fear is only an emotion, just like any other emotion and needs to be managed.**

To manage fear, we need to understand fear. Fear is a reaction that is birthed in our own minds. Yes, fear is real, but it is, in fact, a real emotional response to a situation that had you on alert. In my experience, I believe there are healthy fears and unhealthy fears.

If you were swimming in the ocean and suddenly saw a fin approaching you, what would you do? The feeling you experience would determine your outcome. The awareness of the danger would cause you to freeze up and freak out or go on alert and seek a positive solution.

Healthy fears are based on a previous experience or idea that has caused us to create an awareness of a negative end result. We have reconciled with it and believe that we are prepared to manage through it. Because of this previous experience, we take action to avoid another negative end result by taking control of our thoughts and actions.

Chapter 4 – Where Do You Start?

Unhealthy fears are based on a previous experience or idea that has caused us to create an awareness of a negative end result that still terrifies us because we don't feel in control. Because of this experience, we don't believe we can take action to avoid another negative end result, our thoughts and actions focus on negative possibilities.

When you consider pursuing a big goal, fear will inevitably enter your mind as a deterrent. You must decide if you will respond with a healthy approach or an unhealthy one. Because you might not be completely engaged and you are emotionally analyzing, unhealthy fear often becomes the prevailing emotion that wins out over your decision to take action.

When you have a desire or you 'want' to do something in your life, you will usually spend more time dreaming about the idea and the potential outcome positively. It's nice to think about a vacation, starting school or going back to school, making more money, losing weight or positively changing your life.

When you are listening to your 'wants,' and you can start to filter out your needs, you are heading down the right path to combat fear. When you 'need' to do something, purpose kicks in and your desire pushes you to have faith to believe that you "can." This mindset can start to diminish your fear because you will no longer focus on the fear, you will focus on the positive outcome. **You will always drown your fear with purposeful action.**

Are you ready to have faith and take action NOW? Then overcome your fear with healthy thoughts. Remember that if you failed in the past, what worked for you in the past, might not have the same impact today or it might not even be relevant. You must become better by overcoming fear. If you want to succeed in life, it is your responsibility to adapt, focus and take action with courage! People who live and o

Chapter 4 – Where Do You Start?

operate with fear as a driver are the primary offenders of the "I can't" "It's not possible" and the negative "What if…" mindset.

This type of mindset can be created and is usually prevalent when we get a negative result that is in line with our comfort zone. We can get a false sense that we are being unproductive, and we might even be unproductive, but not to the standards that are in line with our capabilities. Realistically, it might even make sense to us, but the truth is we are being held down by fear. When something appears not to be working, we might even say, **"Why would I change?"**

The challenge with this mindset is that you are missing out on opportunities; you might miss realizing your full potential. Ironically, those with a fearful mindset know that they are wrong. They know that the true reason they don't want to change lies inside. It is really about an internal challenge to break free from a long habitual comfort level of doing "What I know, What I like and What feels good" and starting towards "What I can become!"

Change is never easy, that's why so many don't do it.

Here are my tips to overcoming fear to get started:

1. Keep an open mind to consider a better way.
2. Ask for and listen to feedback from a mentor.
3. Focus on the positive benefits.
4. Ask, "Do I want to live fearful or purposeful?"
5. Ask, "What if I do? How will that change my life?"
6. Make a decision to get started NOW.
7. Take it one day at a time.
8. Ask, "What will it cost me if I don't start or if I quit?"

Chapter 4 – Where Do You Start?

Starting is never easy; nothing worthwhile ever is, so don't expect results to happen overnight. Stay positive and stay committed to the results, not bound to your feelings of fear, and you can and will eventually succeed.

Your willingness to get started shows you and those close to you much about your character and courage.

How do you see YOU?
Are you willing to get started NOW?

Dealing with Failure
When you decide to take action and go for that job, goal, diet, big dream, etc., you are fired up. You take action, but then you encounter the dreaded "failure." So what do you do after you are punched in the proverbial gut?

You start your recovery by following these 4 tips:

1. **Understand that failure is not personal!**
Although failure feels personal, it really isn't. If you start pursuing an idea, dream, a business plan, etc., when someone tells you "NO" or if you fail, remember that you are only experiencing failure. You, in fact, are not a failure.

2. **Failure is an opportunity to re-evaluate!**
Your thoughts, plans, or ideas may need tweaking, or they may need to be forgotten completely (in some cases); but either way, use the failure as a learning experience.

3. **Know your value!**
Understand that just because some other person fails to see the value in your goal, does not mean that it is not valuable.

Chapter 4 – Where Do You Start?

4. **Get over it and Keep Going!**
Remember, just because you encountered a failure does not mean that YOU are a failure! Stay positive, find your strength and simply move on. Sulking and holding on to failure is a recipe for disaster!

Failure is not meant to define you, it is meant to refine you!

Actions you should take:
Get feedback after your encounter. Talk with someone you trust who might have a better understanding of what didn't happen or what needed to happen. Keep an open mind and find out what you did or did not do and then get started again, NOW.

Share your goals and ideas with a mentor prior to starting them, and again afterward to review the end results. You might be missing something. Look for constructive feedback on adjustments that you can make for maximum effectiveness, or you might be told to kill the idea altogether. It might not be the right (or realistic) plan for you. It might be a want and not a need. The end result is, be proud of yourself for taking action! **For every failure you encounter, always remember there is another chance to win if you just keep going.**

Today is your day, start NOW, at the beginning, with something that is important.

Chapter 4 – Where Do You Start?

Challenge Questions:

Where do you need to start?
_____
_____
_____

Why?
_____
_____

What do you need to overcome to start?
_____
_____

How will you develop discipline to start?
_____
_____

What things cause you to procrastinate?
_____
_____

Chapter 4 – Where Do You Start?

What will you do when you say I'll wait?

_____

_____

Why?

_____

_____

Notes:

_____

_____

_____

_____

_____

_____

"Growth isn't determined by your circumstances.
It's determined by your willingness to
Believe and take action."

Chapter 5
Why Now Is the Best Time

Chapter 5 – Why NOW Is the Best Time

The Value of Time

Last year in January, I was ready to create my best year so far in my life. I was focused and driven to impact as many lives as possible. I was in my second year of my master's program while working full time as a speaker, and life seemed great. For a few weeks earlier, I had been experiencing severe neck and head pain, but being an eternal optimist, I was working through it. I had several tests conducted and was given medicine for pain.

One morning after finishing my work, I noticed the pain had gotten much worse and was starting to radiate up through my head. It was intense and prevented me from sitting up. I took some of the medicine and laid down to rest. The pain lingered the remainder of the day and throughout the week.

The next week I had a seminar in Dallas, so I rested up, took some traditional headache pills and proceed to do what I do best. I felt great during the event, but when I arrived home, I was light-headed and felt faint. The last thing I remember was calling out to my wife. She had to tell me the rest of the story of how I fainted, fell and hit my head in our formal dining room. An ambulance arrived and took me to the ER. They gave me an MRI, an MRA, and a neck CT scan; I never had so many tests performed. I was then admitted to the hospital overnight for additional monitoring.

While I was lying in the bed, it was the first time in a long time that I really had the chance to think about my life direction. I was happy with my life and my career. I had overcome the difficulty of the fear to take the big step years earlier, but this head thing was making me think. The fall itself could have been worse. But why was it happening?

Chapter 5 – Why NOW Is the Best Time

What if this was a big issue? I realized that there was so much in life that I had accomplished, but so much more that I needed to do. I suddenly had a clear awareness of the value of time; My life's time.

I committed to get a resolution on my head matter and then start prioritizing my life. I realized that anything can happen to anyone at any time. The fainting event that I had wasn't ideal, but hey, I was still alive. It wasn't my time, **but I was now aware that I shouldn't delay any more on things I needed to do. Neither should you.**

Now is the best time because it is the time that is happening. That means there is value in your time, in every heartbeat, and your time needs to be used responsibly.

Tomorrow Isn't Promised.

Most of us celebrate our birthdays. They are a time for people to imbibe and celebrate the life they have lived, mostly without thinking about the remaining days to come. When will it all end for you? No one knows, and because of the nature of death, most are afraid to talk about it. Not me. My faith assures me that I have great things to face when I die, but that's another story.

The truth is that you could die today. Many wake up and face that reality with a spouse, a friend or a co-worker. If that last sentence freaked you out, then you are with the majority that are living in denial. Death is certain, accept that. No one knows when their time will come, but it is nothing to fear, and my intent is not to scare you. Instead, my intent is to create awareness for you not to fall into the trap that death is many years away. Hopefully, it is for you, but maybe it isn't.

Chapter 5 – Why NOW Is the Best Time

View the end as a reality that will bookend your birth, and you will be forced to focus on living a better-quality day every day, starting now. The value of your life is important, but it needs to be discovered and treated with respect by you. You might think this is morbid or dark, and I will tell you that you are wrong. If you have ever warned your child not to do something that could potentially hurt or kill them, you used the same concept. Your goal was not to instill fear but to create awareness because you care.

Stop waiting for tomorrow, next month, or next year. Today is here for you now, to maximize your minutes and your precious heartbeats.

The 8 Components to START NOW!

Now is the best time not just because you should value your time, but because when you don't act NOW, you are procrastinating. Prevention by procrastination is self-defeating. **It is an excuse-based mindset driven by being comfortable to avoid pain or by utilizing excuses to offset the fear of failure.** If you want to do anything new or make a change in your life remember these eight components:

1. **Start NOW, or chances are you won't start at all.** The more you delay, the less important your dream or goal will become, until you finally lie to yourself (and others) and say that it isn't important anymore.

Chapter 5 – Why NOW Is the Best Time

2. **When you procrastinate, you are reinforcing your excuses.** A delay is usually due to something out of your control. Procrastination is a self-defeating act you can control. Accept that you are procrastinating, figure out why and then start NOW.

3. **Don't hide your procrastination by saying you are planning or preparing.** If this is you, you are still in the 'want' stage. You need to figure out if you 'NEED' to pursue your dream or goal. I'm not saying not to plan or prepare, they are important, but they mean nothing without action. Don't over-plan or over-prepare. Establish a deadline and go.

4. **Remember why you are starting NOW in the first place.** You don't get braces to create pain in your teeth; you get braces to have straight teeth. When your journey becomes painful (it will), then you must remember the goal, your reason why, and not focus on the pain of the task.

5. **Pain that accompanies new action can be good. If you believe it is.** You must experience labor pains in order to have a baby, you must have muscle fatigue to build the muscle, and you must experience personal pain to grow in your life. Not physical pain, but the pain of doing something new, of change and of creating new routines. This is normal and critical to go through, so you can grow.

Chapter 5 – Why NOW Is the Best Time

6. **Not starting means losing something.**
When you don't start you lose time, experience, hope, and maybe even your true purpose. Is it worth it to you?

7. **Failure is a requirement for success.**
Failure is an equal, necessary and important part of success. You must experience failures many times before you can succeed. This must happen so you can learn what not to do and what needs to be done. **If you avoid failure, then you have already failed because you are preventing success.**

8. **Get Uncomfortable.** Most people will miss out on their big goals, simply because they will do what they want to do and stay comfortable, afraid of being uncomfortable. Remember that **in order to be effective, you must be willing to get uncomfortable.**

Be Responsible.
"Ok Mike, I've always wanted to be a Rockstar, so I'm doing it now, quitting my job and seeing where the road takes me!"

My friend that is not a mindset of NOW, that's is a mindset of WOAH! Don't be stupid. There is a big difference between responsibly acting on your big goals NOW and irresponsibly pursuing an unqualified dream.

Chapter 5 – Why NOW Is the Best Time

(You should start the book over if you don't understand this).

Your motivation should not be just to jump into anything or to jump in unprepared. That is NOT what I am teaching in this book. Your motivation should be to understand that having a mindset of NOW means that you purposely know why you need to act on your goal.

You need to responsibly manage what you are called to pursue, by doing these things:

1. Sit down NOW and know and accept your big calling(s) that you need to do, to get you where you need to go. Know WHY you need to do it.
2. Know what will be required financially.
3. Identify the fears, doubts, excuses, and people that will prevent you from taking action.
4. Understand how much time will be required.
5. Know what it will cost you or what it is costing you now (opportunity cost).
6. Learn what you can adjust or remove from your life to create time for your new plan.
7. Understand the skill set needed to gain or grow.
8. Know the people you need to talk with for wise insight.
9. Identify the actions that you need to take NOW!
10. Have the courage to take the first step NOW!

Chapter 5 – Why NOW Is the Best Time

REQUIREMENTS FOR SUCCESS

All of these following questions must be answered: YES or NO only. Understand that ALL of these work together as a complete package. ('Maybe' or, 'kind of' means NO).

1. **Do I LOVE what I believe I am called to do?**
   If you don't love it, you won't commit. You won't do what is necessary for the best possible outcome. You will quit when things get tough or, you will never get started.
2. **Am I really good at it?**
   If you aren't really good at it, you cannot create an impact. If you don't love it, you won't work to get better to become your best at it.
3. **Is there a NEED for it in this world?**
   This is how you change lives and how you earn a living. If there isn't a need for it, it doesn't matter how good you are; you can't have an impact. When you help others due to a need, you can earn a living.
4. **Are you taking action?**
   Are you doing it NOW?
5. **Are you putting your life foundation (God) first?**
   Without God first, you will be misguided and pursue the wrong thing, or you will get distracted on the wrong things.

Again, all of these 5 principles must work together. If you don't love what you are going to do NOW, you won't put in the required effort to develop your skillset to get better. If you aren't good at it, then you cannot fill a need. If there isn't a need for it, then you cannot make a living. If you aren't putting God first, chances are you are focused on the wrong outcome, and starting for the wrong reasons. Finally, if you aren't taking action NOW, it will never happen for you.

Chapter 5 – Why NOW Is the Best Time

MOTIVATION

So, what motivates you and how will you stay powered up!

A battery has two polarities that are required for it to power up so it can do its job. If a battery has two positives or two negatives, it won't work, or it will explode. As people, we can borrow this concept to power up and live our best life. We need to have both positive and negative motivation in order to succeed and pursue our big goals.

POSITIVE MOTIVATION is knowing what you will gain or become.

This means that you have determined what is the most important thing(s) to you in your life right now. What you can gain, become and create an impact in this world. They are important enough to inspire you to take BIG action AND not give up. Your positive motivation should be powerful enough to push you through when you are tired, feeling down or tempted to quit. This isn't superficial motivation; it is life impacting. It inspires you because you know how the positive outcome will benefit you and others in your life. Positive motivation can and should be different for everyone, because what is important to you, might not be important to others, and vice versa. I have known people who were motivated by material gain: to buy a home, a car or to have money in the bank. Others wanted to pay for college, go on a dream trip, get married or live on their own terms. The key here is that you must decide what powerfully motivates you to do what you need to do, NOW!

Chapter 5 – Why NOW Is the Best Time

NEGATIVE Motivation is what inspires you to prevent what you DON'T want to happen.

Some stay focused because they need to stay on the right track in life. They have been in a bad place, and they NEVER want to go back, or they want to avoid going there completely. This is called negative motivation.

I had an employee who worked for me who was constantly in the office before everyone else and was the last one out. He didn't have the talent level of the top performers, his clothes were not designer brands, but his work ethic was second to none. He was inspired to perform.

One day when I was leaving the office, he walked out with me. I told him that I respected how hard he worked, and I asked him what was inspiring him. He told me that he was working to get out of debt to build a better life for his younger kids. He told me that he had learned his lesson about getting in debt and he was convicted not to let his children bear the weight of his bad finances. He would never be in that situation again. This man had true, purposeful negative motivation.
It was life-impacting to him.

What about you?
What would you like to stop happening in your life or what would you like to prevent from happening again? Is it painful enough for you that you will do what it takes to keep you far away from it? What would you like to gain? What are you working for and towards? Is it big enough to sustain your efforts? If not, maybe its just a dream, an interest, and not a life-changing purpose. Maybe it is, and you're not willing to pay the price (opportunity cost) to make it happen.

Chapter 5 – Why NOW Is the Best Time

The Four Pillars

At this point, it is easy to point blame, make excuses or declare why none of this content is applicable to you. Please don't. I have had the great privilege to work with a variety of people all over the globe. From millionaires to broke and unemployed people, I can tell you with complete certainty that everyone in the world is facing or has faced some type of life challenge. The major catalyst that determines a person's outcome is how they deal with the challenge they are facing. While some are impacted positively to move up and on, others are devastated and move out or down. A successful outcome isn't determined by the situation, or the event, it's always about the person and how they choose to deal with what happens.

I have learned that **a life challenge that might destroy one person can easily be a stepping stone that another uses to become stronger.**

When we experience life issues, some falsely say that their life is falling apart. I often say **"maybe your life isn't falling apart; maybe it's coming together in a new way."**

There are really 4 primary "pillars" that we have in our lives that we tend to rely on for our safety and security and most importantly, our happiness. When any of these pillars are affected in any way, they logically and normally create major stress for us and affect our happiness. This is an incorrect way you live.

Chapter 5 – Why NOW Is the Best Time

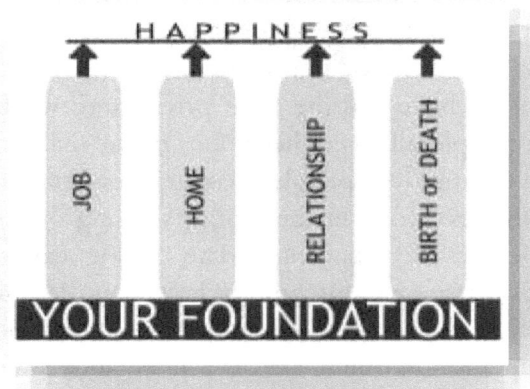

The Four Major Stressors in life involve changing anyone of your core, four pillars. There are obviously other stressors, but these have the greatest impact.

1. **Change in job/career/school**
   If you lose your job, start a new job or change your career, you will feel stressed about your direction and financial security. We rely on an income to survive, but many of us compromise our life-long goals for the comfort of money. It is a compromise few can afford to live with.

2. **Change in home (where you live)**
   When you move, buy a new home, leave or lose your current home, you are going to feel stressed. Everyone must live somewhere, but a home is truly where you make it. It is stressful to leave your comfort zone, but it should be more stressful to let it define you.

3. **Change in relationship**

    If you start a new relationship, have trouble in a current relationship, separate, break up, or divorce, you are going to feel stressed about many things emotionally and materially. You must give yourself time to heal and figure out yourself on your own. You will need to focus on your life value.

4. **Birth or death (Health falls into this category)**

    If someone close to you dies, if you have a terminal illness, or if you and your spouse find out you are having a child, you are going to feel emotionally empty or emotionally overwhelmed. A new life or a loss of life is a big deal. Choose to celebrate all life. You must heal and start moving on.

When you experience a major change with one, multiple, or all of these pillars, picture your pillar, cracking, crumbling or falling down, leaving a dust pile. The reality is that you are going to feel very stressed, and that is normal. However, it is not normal for you to stay stressed. When these major changes to our pillars occur, this is when we falsely say "My life is falling apart," only because we have a weak foundation and we rely on the pillars to provide our happiness. When a pillar that we have relied on for happiness is destroyed, our happiness will be destroyed.

Chapter 5 – Why NOW Is the Best Time

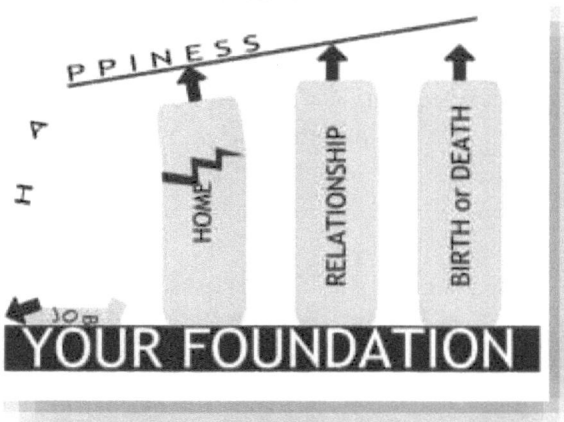

Although it might feel like your life is falling apart, and happiness has left you, the reality is that you have a pillar(s) that has been destroyed and it (or they) need to be rebuilt. This is where it gets tough for us because rebuilding a pillar is very difficult, but they must be rebuilt.

Because of the unhappiness, stress, and level of difficulty, some will not look for the appropriate strength to rebuild. They will be left with a life of sorrow, regret, and blame. Others will try to take control of their own life and will get frustrated trying to rebuild a replica of what was torn down. Some will get frustrated and give up on the task that they aren't equipped to handle.

Know that **when your pillar or pillars are knocked down, this is your opportunity to evaluate your life foundation.**

Chapter 5 – Why NOW Is the Best Time

What are you building on?

Your life foundation is what your pillars rest on. When your pillars get knocked down, you can rebuild if your foundation is strong enough. For me and others who have experienced many events with our pillars being destroyed, we finally realized that we weren't strong enough and we placed our trust in Christ to be our life foundation. The secret here is that happiness doesn't come from things, happiness comes from your life foundation.

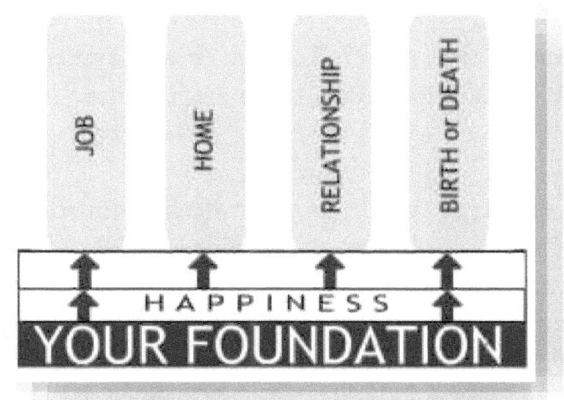

With a strong foundation, you are better prepared to handle life's biggest challenges. If you show up to work and learn you are laid off, then you leave to go home and find that your house was foreclosed on, your wife decided to leave because of the stress, and your daughter announces that she is having a baby. Yes, you will be stressed. But know this, your life is not over. You can and will rebuild if your foundation is strong enough.

Chapter 5 – Why NOW Is the Best Time

With a strong foundation of faith, you can use this opportunity to start NOW and pursue that new career you've always wanted. You can find a new place to live, you can reconcile with your wife, and you can enjoy the new life that you have been blessed with in your new grandbaby. Happiness through faith will drive you to move on.

Without a strong foundation, you will feel the weight personally. And if you are finding your happiness in things, your happiness will go when your things are gone. My friend, you aren't strong enough to handle these types of events on your own. For some of you, these are precisely the types of events that have happened to you that are preventing you from taking action NOW. You haven't recovered, because you don't have a foundation, or your foundation isn't strong enough. They are holing you back.

What are you relying on as your life foundation?

Where you are in your spiritual walk is critical to establishing your vision and your outcomes. You didn't create yourself, so you need to know who created you and start building that relationship NOW. Don't believe what you want to believe, seek the truth and believe what you need to believe. The truth will set you free. Your spiritual faith needs to be the foundation of your life. Just as every solid structure has a strong foundation, your spiritual life needs to be your solid foundation. If a storm knocks down a building with a strong foundation, the owners can rebuild. When you have a strong foundation, and a storm hits your life and knocks you down, you can also rebuild, by relying on your foundation of faith in Christ. (Yes, I am preaching to you, that's what I am called to do.)

Chapter 5 – Why NOW Is the Best Time

A Mindset of NOW

When you have a mindset of NOW, you don't focus too long on what has happened in our life. You grieve, start healing, start thinking differently, and you focus on:

- Why it happened?
- What you can do differently next time
- What you are going to do to move on
- How you are going to move on
- Who or what you are relying on for strength to move on
- Taking action to move on

Challenge Questions:

What is motivating you positively?

_____
_____
_____

What is motivating you negatively?

_____
_____

What do you spend the majority of your time doing?

_____
_____

Chapter 5 – Why NOW Is the Best Time

What do you rely on for your life foundation?
_____
_____

Why?
_____
_____

Why is now the best time for YOU to start?
_____
_____

What will keep you from starting?
_____
_____

Notes:
_____
_____
_____
_____
_____
_____
_____

"Hope happens when you remember WHY you are doing what you are doing. DON'T QUIT."

Chapter 6
Keep Remembering WHY Not What

Chapter 6 – Keep Remembering WHY Not What

One of the biggest challenges that you will face each day when you start a new direction is staying the course. This can only be accomplished by evaluating your mindset. Your mind is a powerful tool. What you say is a reflection of what you have trained yourself to accept and believe. When it comes to acting on a dream or goal, this same rule applies and ultimately will determine your level of success.

Working with people around the world, I have proven that people with purpose become more, because they do more, by following the #1 rule of life: they believe more. This rule is reinforced and remembered often. They believe that they are working for something more and that by doing more, they can get closer to accomplishing more. Therefore, they can realize their biggest dreams. By taking daily action and polishing their skills, these people gain tremendous, long-term benefits. In addition, they understand that when they prioritize and focus their mind on purpose, they will lead with powerful, impacting actions. I teach people that your direction in life starts with your belief system.

What you believe is what you will follow.
For example:
If you have convinced yourself that something is too hard, it will become too hard…. for you! Or in contrast, if you believe that you CAN become more, or that you can even do more than you are doing now, then by default, eventually you will make it happen. You can do it as you continue to use the strategies in this book. Either way, true results can only start when your mind is engaged with your reason and your results. Otherwise, you will focus on the daily tasks, which aren't enough to keep you going.

Chapter 6 – Keep Remembering WHY Not What

What about you? How is your mindset?

Are you open to learning new strategies and techniques, or are you just looking for a magical event to happen someday?

Do you really want to become better or are you already prepared with your (or others) life-long excuses that perpetuate a negative mindset? If so, this will drastically impact how you view life, which will poorly affect your interactions with yourself and other people. People with no purpose say negative things which are very telling about their mindset. Inevitably, they will cause other people to focus on and believe their master phrase:

"This is just the way I am!"

I often tell people to pay less attention to the words people use and more attention to why they are using them. If you follow my advice, you can clearly see that anyone who says, "This is the way I am," is really saying, I am stubborn, and I refuse to have an open mindset.

Let me clarify that it is perfectly acceptable for someone to use this phrase if they are *consistently* living their life in a positive and constructive way.

The point is that the key to determining if taking action WILL WORK or WON'T WORK, completely lies in the mind of the person. Change will become what you believe because you will always find what you are looking. If you have convinced yourself that change won't work, then it won't work. Not because it can't, but because you won't let it happen. This is a very true and profound statement that I challenge you to think through.

Chapter 6 – Keep Remembering WHY Not What

BEe where you are

At this point, you need to decide if you are 'all in' and if you are ready to get serious about taking action NOW. I often tell people to "BEe where you are!" (Not a typo, I'll explain) When it comes to action, this rule is a life and career changer.

BEe stands for:
B- brain,
E-eyes and
e-ears.

You need all three to work together to be an effective person.

This might sound easy, but for most of us, we usually aren't where we are supposed to be, which is a result of our distracted mindsets. Let me explain what I mean:

Chapter 6 – Keep Remembering WHY Not What

When I was at work, my body was there, but my mind was usually at home. As a result, my mind beckoned my body to come home. Since my body was at work and my mind wasn't, I couldn't perform in an effective manner. Your brain, eyes, ears, and body, perform best when they are all working together. For me, I simply needed to engage my mind to be at work with my body.

Because of being unfocused, many people today aren't where they are supposed to be. When they are at work, their body is there, but their mind is thinking of other things. Then, when they are at home, their mind is usually somewhere else. Sometimes it's back at work, regretting all of the work that wasn't completed during the day. This insanity repeats itself each day.

To BEe where you are, means being present. It requires you to create transition times, to allow your mind and body to get back in sync from where you were, to where you are now. Effective living requires all of your senses. You need to engage your brain on your daily results, focus your eyes on your current environment, and use your ears to listen to what is going on around you.

Remember WHY you are doing what you are doing. Change your view of daily tasks to view them as daily building blocks.

- ✓ When you are at work BEe there.
- ✓ When you are at home, BEe there.
- ✓ When you decide to start, start NOW and BEe there.

Chapter 6 – Keep Remembering WHY Not What

This strategy, to 'be present,' can and will be a game changer for you. You will get more out of your job, your family, your relationships, and your life.

Continue to Build Your Dream Foundations
Earlier I spoke about building your life foundation. Your dream foundations are the decisive and purposeful actions that you take to build towards your biggest goals. My foundations to pursue my lifelong dreams and goals are clear, defined and profound, but they haven't always been that way.

When I was a senior in high school, I had a teacher who believed in me. On the last day of school, she called me up to the front of the class, and she handed me an envelope. I went back to my desk and opened it and read the contents on the paper inside, written in red calligraphy:

> "If you have
> built castles
> in the air,
> your work
> need not be
> lost; that is
> where they
> should be.
> Now put the
> foundations
> under them.
>
> - Henry David Thoreau
>
> Congratulations!
> - Mrs. Brown."

Chapter 6 – Keep Remembering WHY Not What

I thought the note was wonderful. I did have castles in the air (dreams), and it now was apparent that in order for those castles to be realized I need to make them happen. But how? I didn't have the answers, so I went home and gave the envelope to my mom. I just assumed that she would do something with it.

I didn't realize it at the time, but Mrs. Brown had planted a seed in my mind that was growing towards helping me to understand my WHY, my purpose. Although I didn't know where the note was, I kept that note and its contents in my mind and would recall those powerful words, whenever I felt I needed to pursue and build my biggest castles (dreams). I would then know that I needed to start building foundations under them to make them real; otherwise, they would stay images in my mind. Each time I knew that I needed to act NOW.

About 30 years after that event, I went to visit my now retired parents. During our visit, while talking about life and things important to us, my mother said, "Oh, by the way, I have something for you. I have always kept it and wanted to give it to you." She stood up and went into the other room. When she came back, she was holding the envelope that Mrs. Brown had given to me. I opened it up and read those words that I had planted in my mind three decades earlier. Those words that had grown from a seed into a part of who I was. I had become a builder. Now, as a man with a family, I had the opportunity to look back on all of the foundations that I had taken action to build to make my biggest dreams come true. I was a speaker, I was an author, I was a great father, I was sober, and I was taking action to preach globally.

Chapter 6 – Keep Remembering WHY Not What

It was powerful and fulfilling to see God's hand at work, going from the mind of a lost and confused 18-year-old, to a man who was living his calling, simply by having faith and by taking purposeful action.

You see every time I wanted to give up; I remembered WHY I was doing what I was doing. I knew that if I quit, that it was over, and the castles would never be built. I knew that I couldn't live with that outcome. For me, I knew what God had given me. I knew that I needed to be a good steward of not only my dreams, but of my attitude, faith, and actions, so I kept going, and I will always keep going, by acting NOW.

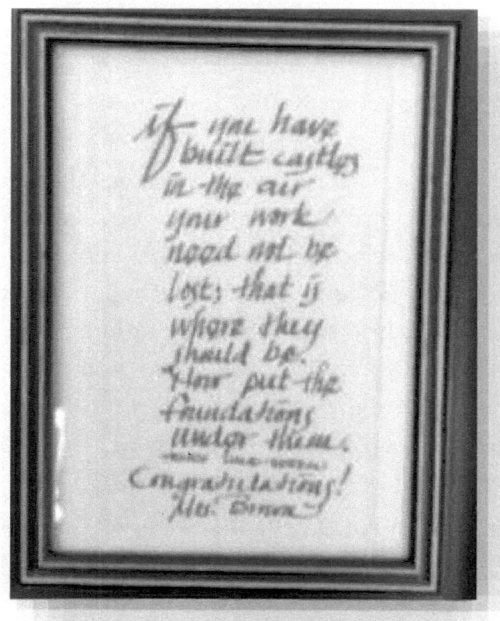

The actual note from Mrs. Brown, framed and in my office.

Chapter 6 – Keep Remembering WHY Not What

What about you?
- ❖ What will push you to start NOW?
- ❖ What is going to keep you from quitting?
- ❖ What will help you back up when you get knocked down?
- ❖ What will keep you going, when it gets tough?
- ❖ What will keep you focused when you get distracted?

When you focus on WHAT you are doing, it becomes a task. When you remember WHY you are doing what you are doing, it becomes a meaningful purpose. Completing a task every day does not create enough purpose to push you through; purpose will always keep you going.

Challenge Questions:

How do you view your life NOW?
_____
_____
_____

Are you happy where you are?
_____

Have you decided where you are going?
_____

Chapter 6 – Keep Remembering WHY Not What

Who do you commit to becoming?
_____

Are you capable of becoming more?
_____

When will you start?
_____

WHY?
_____

Chapter 6 – Keep Remembering WHY Not What

> "Many can live through the pain of
> pursuing their biggest dreams,
> no one can live with regret."

Chapter 7 – I Challenge YOU

> "Trying shows a lack of commitment; commit and find a way."

Chapter 7
I Challenge You.

Chapter 7 – I Challenge YOU

I always say that "Through faith and action, all things are possible," and I really believe it. Mostly because I have experienced it and I keep seeing it happen first hand. Every time I falsely believed something couldn't happen for me, it didn't. I simply didn't take action. It made me mad to think that I was creating my own negative outcome. We all do it or have done it. Are you doing it now?

As of the writing of this book, I am currently challenging myself by studying full-time for my master's degree at seminary to preach globally. Please know that I'm not bragging, this is a part of the concepts you have read about in this book. Let me explain.

I dropped out of college because it wasn't important to me, so I didn't finish my undergraduate degree. I couldn't see the big picture, so it seemed like pursuing it was a waste of time. I had just graduated high school and realized that having to attend more school while paying for it was a new concept that just didn't make sense. I was a go-getter, working two jobs and going to school full-time. At that time, additional schooling just didn't have value and therefore wasn't important to me. I quickly concluded that my direction in life didn't include more classroom time, so I decided to leave.

When I announced my plans, I was told by many that it wasn't the right time to do something drastic like that. They were right. What I didn't comprehend back then in my naïve mind was that I wasn't going to school to pay for classes, I was going to school for an education. College was an investment in myself to prepare me to succeed in my life. I had it backwards. I did have a purpose, but I didn't have a purpose for school; therefore I wasn't giving my best. I was wasting my time and money. Soon after, I pursued a career in retail to become a manager.

Chapter 7 – I Challenge YOU

I had a new purpose. I was misguided and driven by money and title, but I didn't see that at the time. I worked extremely hard, and I was quickly promoted into management. At age 20, I received my own jewelry store in Dallas. After attaining that goal, I knew that there had to be more important things out there for me. Store management was no longer a priority, so I decided to leave the retail business.

At that same time in my life, I met Bonnie. She understood me, we connected. She believed in me and unconditionally supported me. I was inspired, so I left my management job to start my new career direction, all to the voices of many saying, "It isn't the right time to be leaving."

Only a few short months after dating each other, I knew that Bonnie was the girl for me. She was very important to me. Five months later, to the surprise of everyone, we got married. We both knew it was the right time, but the timing didn't sit well with many people that we knew.

During the few months before our marriage, it was important for me to get on a better career path, so I applied for a job in telecom. This new job was only slightly better than my current employment, which was straight commission. I was fortunate enough to get hired. Many people informed me that it wasn't the right time to be starting a new career right before getting married. I viewed it differently. I was making positive change by getting married and starting a new job. When I accepted the job, the employer let me know that my start date would be Monday, October 14. Bonnie and I were getting married on Sunday, October 13. Many people told us it wasn't the best time. They said we were getting married too soon and that it wasn't good to start work right after a wedding. They said we should be taking a honeymoon, but we couldn't afford one, and I was driven to start my new direction.

Chapter 7 – I Challenge YOU

Each time we took action, we received the same response: Are you sure it's the best time? I would change telecom jobs again. Every time we made a change, we heard those same words questioning us about it being 'the best time.'

Although this book isn't an autobiography, my life is a great example of the NOW principle at work successfully. When I look back on my life, I can see that although it might not have been the 'right' time for some of those events to take place, it was always the 'best time.'

To the concern of most people, I did take action to keep going. I overcame and often succeeded. I can also say that although the timing might have been concerning to some, every one of those events where I acted NOW, was a major blessing in my life. They have been stepping stones to new events that have led me to become more. That first telecom job led to a successful twenty-five-year career in telecom, which built credentials that lead me to my career as a speaker and author, and on to where God leads me next.

Acting NOW doesn't mean you won't take the wrong step.

I can now see and understand what I saw back then and why I acted. Every time I made a serious move, it was because it was critically important to me and Bonnie. It was setting our course in life. I somehow recognized that I needed to do what needed to be done. Not just out of selfish ambition, but because I knew the action or event needed to be pursued to help us with the direction of our lives. I somehow felt that the risk was necessary to start the path. Each step was necessary. Sometimes they were a wrong step, but it was always the best time to take the step.

Chapter 7 – I Challenge YOU

I knew that if I didn't act for fear of taking the wrong step, that I would never take a single step, and that frightened me more.

I eventually learned and made corrections and adjustments. Each move required a specific effort to prepare me for the next move; therefore every move was important.

So yes, I dropped out of college, and now I'm pursuing my master's degree, while I speak full-time. This is all 100% due to my faith, a mindset of NOW, overcoming failure and building new successes that have gotten me to where I am. I simply stopped focusing on what couldn't be done and started focusing on what could be done. My philosophy is that if someone else could do it, and God wants me to do it, I can succeed. So can you.

Yes, it has been hard, but not impossible. Please know that there isn't anything special about me. How did it happen you say? Faith and action, that's how. I saw opportunity and acted on it. If I can do it, so can you.

I Challenge You

In my book Lion leadership, I wrote about how in a lion pride when one member decides that they want to lead, they will challenge the leader. When this happens, the challenger has reached a point in their life and their mind that they believe they are capable, prepared, and ready. The only obstacle that stands in the way is their ability to defeat the existing leader. Their belief system must be validated, so they will decide to pursue the coveted spot, and at some point, they will decide to take action.

Chapter 7 – I Challenge YOU

I challenge you to replace your doubts and fears with a mindset of NOW.
What you believe is what you will follow. Know what you are following, understand why, and ensure you are following the right things. Believe that you are capable. Know that you are ready to move your life and your career to the next level. Refuse to think self-doubting thoughts. Be a forward thinker, constantly looking to improve because you believe you can, you know you are worthy, and you know that NOW is the time to act.

I challenge you to break your routines of being complacent.
Every person has established life and work routines. Yours might have been holding you back, but not anymore. Commit today to start new routines that will take you closer to your goals. Recognize that just because you have been doing something for a long time that you no longer have an excuse to accept it as being right. Just because you have been getting a good result, doesn't mean it's the best way. Recognize and eliminate complacent actions.

I challenge you to figure out what is important to you.
You may be at a point in your life or career that you don't want to be. Know that you can change if you desire to stop giving your valuable time to things and people that aren't important to you. Realize what is important to you and start doing activities that invest in the things and people that really matter to you. Know what needs to be the most important.

Chapter 7 – I Challenge YOU

I challenge you to stay focused.
This means that your mind and eyes will keep a priority on the long term prize you desire. Refocus every morning and relax every night after reviewing your day. Know that if you are performing at your best level, at the best possible moments, then you don't have to worry about anyone else. Don't focus on distractions, keep your eyes on your goal.

I challenge you to rethink your belief system.
Start believing in your purpose and your foundation. Accept that you are capable and ready to get started. You may not be an expert today, but you will be if you believe it and make it happen. Think about ways to change and improve your life, the lives of others, and the ultimate legacy you leave behind. Believe it can happen for you and start NOW.

I challenge you to no longer negotiate with mediocrity and procrastination.
Eliminate these major problems from your life. Hang around others with a mindset of NOW, who desire to become better, by ensuring that they have everything they need to succeed. Develop your weaknesses by taking time for personal development Refuse to accept excuses, blame, negativity or mediocrity. Recognize that these are symptoms of failure and create an unhealthy mindset. They damage performance. Do not tolerate or accept anything that will compromise the success of your dreams or your faith.

I challenge you to take action NOW.
People with the mindset of NOW are respected, trusted and loved. They help others to discover their courage

Chapter 7 – I Challenge YOU

and to shed their skins of complacency. They establish a vision and help others to realize and believe without a doubt. They inspire others to pursue excellence with complete and unquestioned accountability. They find a way when no one else can see a way. They rise after everyone else has fallen. Their power and strength from their life foundation are manifested in the way they carry themselves, through humbled strength. They pursue the vision and exceed the expectations of what they were born to do. Never forget that living your life is a privilege and an honor that few embrace properly, but not you.

Living life with a mindset of NOW requires courage and is not for the weak. Even the Bible reminds us: "To whom much is given, much is expected." Remember that taking action NOW is a responsibility that you should respect and never abuse. Don't jump into things blindly or for the wrong reasons. Seek wise counsel from those you trust and ignore those who seek to prevent you from attaining your big goals or will lead you astray.

When you apply the principles in this book, you will get resistance as you struggle with your new vision. After time, challenges, and tests of endurance, others will come to respect you and love you and what you represent. We aren't living to please others; we are living to set a better example.

Don't be afraid to create disruptive change when necessary. People will emotionally deflect and hide behind the false claims of their dislike for your new discipline and drive. What they really dislike is the new accountability to perform and the expectations to step outside of their mediocrity. Stretch your comfort zone.

Chapter 7 – I Challenge YOU

Whatever your current situation is, know that you now have everything you need to start your journey towards success. You just need to recognize it and own it.

As you start using the strategies contained in this book, you can effectively change the outcome of your results, your career, the course of your life and the lives of others.

I challenge you and ask you to embrace a mindset of NOW to pursue your true purpose and your life calling. The best time to start is NOW.

I have challenged you.

What will you do?

I accept the challenge to create a mindset of NOW:

_____

Signed

_____

Date

Chapter 7 – I Challenge YOU

Chapter 7 – I Challenge YOU

"Success starts when your actions become greater than your excuses."
- Mike Rodriguez

Chapter 7 – I Challenge YOU

Conclusion

I have always enjoyed my life, but I was not always in pursuit of becoming the best me; mostly because I was my biggest obstacle. I was often distracted by doing things my way or by people and things that kept me from stepping into my full potential. I knew I should "act NOW," I was just not focused enough to do it. As a result, I dealt with the repercussions through a lack of engagement, and poor results, until I decided to take action to improve. However, I only took action to improve, when I chose to be aware of my ineffective skills and to seek out guidance from mentors. I came to understand the purpose of being an effective person, and I became stronger than ever. Not in a controlling way, but in a humbled position of silent strength.

I have learned, through failure and success, that I must be healthy in three categories: spiritually, mentally and physically. These core life components will always be works in progress for me. However, I am committed to my success. With regards to success, I have always felt that my purpose was to help others through the gift of words. I have always dreamed of becoming a professional speaker and trainer, but for the largest part of my life, I only considered this a dream. Who was I to accomplish this? This was a negative thought that I burdened myself with. So, who am I? I am a son of our King. I know Him, and He knows me. Today, all because of Him, and through my obedience of acting NOW, I am living my biggest dreams and most importantly, my life's purpose. Discover God, believe in and receive Jesus and accept Him as your foundation. Have faith and take action. Do it now.

NOW Is the Best Time

NOW Is the Best Time

NOW Is the Best Time

About the Author

Mike Rodriguez is a professional speaker and CEO of Mike Rodriguez International, LLC a global speaking and training firm. Mike is also a Multi-Best-Selling Author, with many of his books featured at Barnes & Noble book events. He is a world-renowned motivator and a people, leadership and sales expert. Mike has co-hosted training alongside the legendary Tom Hopkins, and he is a former showcase speaker with the world-famous Zig Ziglar Corporation. He was selected as the featured speaker and sales expert for their 2015 Ziglar U.S. Tour and is now featured on Amazon Alexa "Inspire Me."

Mike has been featured on CBS, U.S. News & World Report, Fast Company, Success Magazine and many more. He has lectured at Baylor University School of Business, UNT, K-State Research, and UGA. His clients include names like Bank of America, Reuters News Agency, Hilton, McDonalds's Corporation, Little Caesars Pizza, the US Army, the Federal Government, and many others. As a master trainer, Mike has worked with thousands around the globe.

Mike is a high-energy professional who worked in corporate America for well over two decades training, building, mentoring, and developing top performing people and teams. Mike started as a struggling sales representative, with no experience or formal training. He worked his way up to become a top performer and an award-winning sales leader. He credits his faith, having a plan, taking action, and never giving up for enabling him to prevail over many failures and adversities in his own life. Most importantly, he has always believed in his God-given potential.

Throughout his career, Mike has built productivity-driven training programs and managed multi-million-dollar quotas. He has experience delivering powerful messages and creating personal development strategies for new and tenured companies and teams across many industries.

Mike believes if you have the right attitude, you can have the right kind of success, regardless of the type of industry that you are in. Mike has been happily married since 1991 to the love of his life, and together they have five beautiful daughters. As a Pastor in training, Mike has studied Christian Leadership in a Graduate Program at DTS, and he is currently pursuing his Master's Degree (MDiv) at SWBTS.

NOW Is the Best Time

NOW Is the Best Time

As a highly sought-after speaker,
Mike has experience working with people
from all backgrounds, personally and professionally,
all around the world.

You can schedule Mike Rodriguez
to speak or train at your next event.
Go to:
www.MikeRodriguezInternational.com

Other books available by Mike Rodriguez:

Lion Leadership
Finding Your WHY
8 Keys to Exceptional Selling
Break Your Routines to Fix Your Life
Think BIG Motivational Quotes
Plus many Co-Authored Books

Audio Courses (MP3/CD) Available from:
Nightingale Conant and Audible:

What's Holding Me Back?
The Power of Breaking Routines

NOW Is the Best Time

NOW Is the Best Time

NOW Is the Best Time

NOW Is the Best Time

NOW Is the Best Time

Disclaimer & Copyright Information

The information contained in this book is not to be considered medical, physiological or psychiatric advice, nor is the content intended to offer a cure, a course of treatment or a substitute for medical assistance. Please consult your doctor or a medical professional for any medical matter(s) affecting you or someone else, including depression, addiction, suicide or other illnesses.

Some of the events, locales, and conversations have been recreated from memories. In order to maintain their anonymity, in some instances, the names of individuals and places have been changed. As such, some identifying characteristics and details may have changed. All content is original, and any similar instances should be considered a coincidence.

Although the author and publisher have made every effort to ensure that the information in this book was correct at press time, the author and publisher do not assume and hereby disclaim any liability to any party for any loss, damage, or disruption caused by errors or omissions, whether such errors or omissions result from negligence, accident, or any other cause.

All quotes, unless otherwise noted,
are attributed to Mike Rodriguez.

Cover illustration, book design, and production
Copyright © 2019 by Tribute Publishing LLC
www.TributePublishing.com

"Go Forth and Make Your Life Exceptional" ™
is a copyrighted trademark of the Author, Mike Rodriguez.

NOW Is the Best Time

NOW Is the Best Time

NOW Is the Best Time

I can do ALL THINGS through Christ
who strengthens me.
Philippians 4:13

NOW Is the Best Time

NOW Is the Best Time

………..now go forth and start NOW.

It's the best time.

NOW Is the Best Time

NOW Is the Best Time

NOW Is the Best Time

www.ingramcontent.com/pod-product-compliance
Lightning Source LLC
Chambersburg PA
CBHW020425010526
44118CB00010B/430